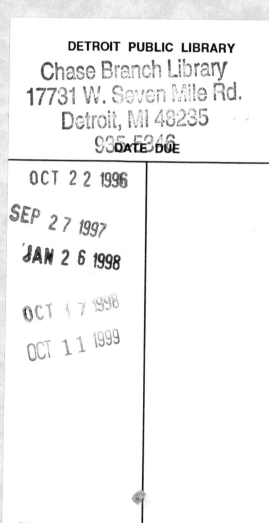

The SEMINOLES
People of the Southeast

TRICIA ANDRYSZEWSKI

NATIVE AMERICANS
THE MILLBROOK PRESS
BROOKFIELD, CONNECTICUT

Cover "Seminole Women Parching Corn" by Fred Beaver. Private Collection, photo courtesy of Native American Painting Reference Library.

Photographs courtesy of Bettmann: pp. 10, 27, 28, 49, 50; National Museum of American Art/Art Resource, NY: pp. 13, 21, 34; Florida State Archives: pp. 17, 19, 24, 31, 41, 46, 48, 53; St. Augustine Historical Society: p. 38; Seminole Nation Historical Society: p. 42; Everglades National Park: pp. 44–45; Florida Department of Commerce, Division of Tourism: p. 55. Map by Joe LeMonnier.

Library of Congress Cataloging-in-Publication Data
Andryszewski, Tricia, 1956–
The Seminoles : people of the Southeast / by Tricia Andryszewski.
p.   cm. — (Native Americans)
Includes bibliographical references and index.
Summary: The history and culture of the Seminoles, who
established themselves in northern Florida in the 1700s,
later moving to the Everglades where many live today.
A traditional recipe and game are included.
ISBN 1-56294-530-0
1. Seminole Indians — History — Juvenile literature.   2. Seminole
Indians — Social life and customs — Juvenile literature.
[1. Seminole Indians.   2. Indians of North America — Florida.]
I. Title.   II. Series.
E99.S28A78   1995
975′.004973 — dc20   94-21819   CIP   AC

Published by The Millbrook Press, Inc.
2 Old New Milford Road, Brookfield, Connecticut 06804

CONTENTS

Facts About the
Traditional Seminole Way of Life
7

Chapter One
The Green Corn Dance
9

Chapter Two
Village Life
16

Chapter Three
Seminoles, Settlers, and Escaped Slaves
25

Chapter Four
The Second Seminole War
33

Chapter Five
Building a New Life
39

Chapter Six
Into the Modern World
51

A Seminole Story:
Rabbit Who Stole the Fire
57

Important Dates 59

Glossary 61

Bibliography 62

Index 63

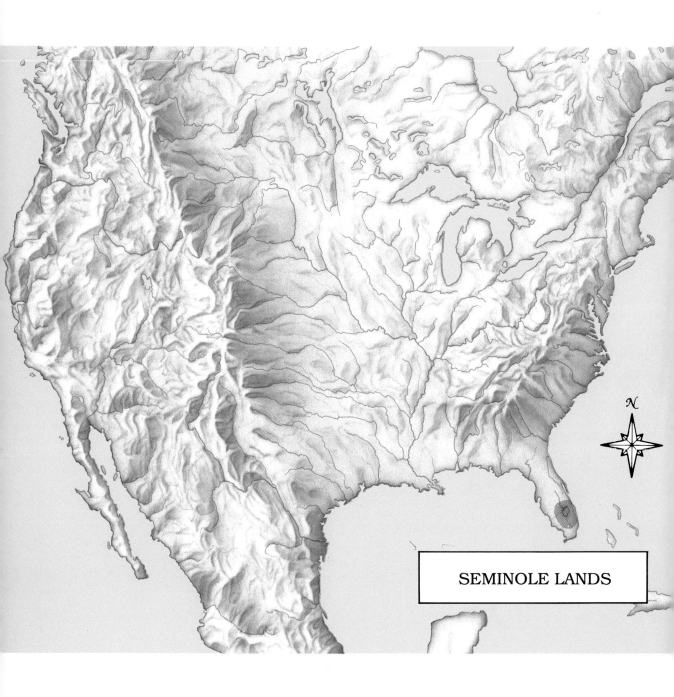

SEMINOLE LANDS

FACTS ABOUT
THE TRADITIONAL SEMINOLE
WAY OF LIFE

GROUP NAME

Seminole

GEOGRAPHIC REGION

Florida

LANGUAGE

Muskogee and Hitchiti

HOUSE TYPE

Wooden huts or open-air chickees

MAIN FOODS

Corn, garden vegetables,
wild plants, fish, and game

Chapter One

THE GREEN CORN DANCE

Early in the summer is when the first corn planted in Florida early in the spring grows sweet and ripe enough to eat. And early in the summer is when the Seminole people of Florida prepared for the Green Corn Dance. This was their most important holiday of the year — a time to visit with friends and family, and to give thanks and celebrate a new harvest of corn, their most important food. The Green Corn Dance was also a time to settle old disagreements, and to make decisions about how the Seminole people should live in the coming year.

Seminoles from many villages gathered at the village where the holiday would be celebrated. Some people gathered wood for the dance fires or cleaned up the area where the dance would take place. Other people repaired the council house, where important meetings were held, or built shelter huts so that everyone coming to the village for the holiday would have a place to sleep. Some of the men and older boys went hunting for food for the holiday feasts.

At the beginning of the holiday festival, men, women, and children danced, played games, and talked with friends and

*An artist's rendering of the Green Corn Dance,
an important part of the traditional and sacred
ceremony of the Seminoles.*

family they had not seen for many months. Everybody ate a feast prepared from dried corn and other food saved from the past year's harvest.

Then the men and older boys began to fast. They would eat no food, but sipped *asi*, the black drink. The Seminoles believed that this strong herbal tea purified their bodies and gave them clear minds for talking about tribal business. It also gave the men strength and energy for the special ceremonial dances.

During this fast, the men met at the council house to talk about crimes that had been committed during the past year, and to decide whether the criminals should be forgiven or punished. The men also discussed other problems facing their people, and tried to agree on solutions to the problems.

Every man present at the council house meeting was encouraged to speak on any matter being discussed, but some men's opinions were respected more than others. The shaman, or medicine man, responsible for overseeing the Green Corn Dance, was especially respected for his religious and medical knowledge. The shaman and several other leaders made up the governing council of the village where the gathering was held. They kept order at the men's meeting in the council house. Leaders from other villages were also listened to carefully, and so were the oldest members of each clan, or group of related families, present at the meeting.

Sometimes — but not every year — there would be a naming ceremony in the council house during the Green Corn Dance. Each boy who took part in the ceremony would be given a new name by the shaman or by the older men of his clan. This naming usually happened when a boy was between twelve and fifteen years old. Receiving this new name meant that he was no longer a little boy but was now a young man and a warrior.

While the Seminole men were meeting at the council house, the women cleared out the village, throwing away old things, and prepared for the great feast to come. The women were also responsible for putting out all of the cooking fires in the village. This was a way of turning out the lights on the old year to make ready for the new. During the men's meeting in the council house, the shaman lit a new fire to bring in the new year. The women took coals from this newly lit fire to restart all the fires in the village.

To light the fire and to perform other ceremonies, the shaman used tools from a sacred medicine bundle. This collection of tools and medicines was the key to the people's well-being, and its power was renewed each year by the Green Corn Dance.

Finally, with the men's business done and the new year officially begun, everyone ate a great feast. The most important part of the meal was the newly harvested fresh sweet corn. This corn was a great treat, because for months dried corn had been the only corn available to eat. After the feast came more dancing and games.

ORIGINS OF THE PEOPLE ▪ The Green Corn Dance is a very old tradition. People in the southeastern part of what is now called the United States gathered for this holiday long before there were Seminoles.

Hundreds of years ago, before explorers from Europe came to Florida, perhaps as many as 100,000 Native Americans lived there. By the 1700s, after the Europeans arrived, these tribes — the Calusas, Apalachees, Timucuas, and others — were almost completely extinct. Many were killed by diseases introduced by the Europeans or during warfare between English and Spanish colonists. Other Native Americans were captured by slave traders. Some moved away from Florida, searching for a safer and healthier place to live.

*Native Americans camp beside the dunes near Pensacola
in northern Florida in this painting by George Catlin.*

Pole Ball Game

The Seminoles were very fond of all kinds of ball games. Men, women, and children all played these games when they gathered for the Green Corn Dance and at other times of the year.

Some games were very rough, played by warriors as a sort of training for battle. But some games were gentler, played by children or by men and women together. Some games were played by large teams of many people, others by just a few players.

One game you can try yourself is the pole ball game.

Players take turns throwing a ball, trying to hit the top of a pole. (Where no pole is available, an outside wall with no windows can be used.)

Find a spot or mark the pole about 25 feet (7.5 meters) up. (The Seminoles used a tall pole with a cow's skull or a wooden fish placed on the top.)

Now find a second spot or mark about 10 feet (3 meters) below the top mark.

Using a small ball, try to hit the top mark. If you do, give yourself 4 points. If your ball hits between the top mark and the bottom mark, give yourself 2 points.

Take turns with your friends.

Thirty points wins the game.

Only a few of these original Floridians remained when Creeks and some other Native Americans began to move into northern Florida. They came from what are now the states of Georgia, Alabama, and the Carolinas. The Creeks' old homelands had become crowded. Much of the best farmland had been exhausted from many years of growing crops, and much of the best game had been hunted. People more and more often fought over these shrinking natural resources. Northern Florida's uncrowded, rich hunting grounds and fertile soil made it an excellent place to settle.

At first the Creeks who moved into Florida tried to maintain friendships, family relations, and a political connection to the Creek Confederacy they had left behind. But communication and transportation in the 1700s were primitive and difficult. Bit by bit, the Florida settlements became an entirely separate culture from—and even hostile to—the northern Creeks. By late in the 1700s the mostly-Creek people of the new Florida settlements were called Seminoles.

VILLAGE LIFE

The early Seminoles of Florida weren't all alike. They didn't even all speak the same language. Most spoke either Muskogee or Hitchiti, two languages about as closely related to each other as French is to Spanish.

The name "Seminole" may have come originally from the Spanish word *cimarrón*, meaning "wild" or "runaway." The Seminoles' own name for themselves was *Ikaniúksalgi*, a Muskogee word meaning "peninsula people."

The first Seminoles settled in parts of northern Florida that had good farmland and reliable sources of drinking water, often by a river or stream. At the center of the village was the council house, where the Green Corn Dance ceremonies and other meetings were held.

FAMILIES ▪ A few early Seminole villages had as many as thirty families, although most had fewer than a dozen. Each family in the village occupied two buildings. One of these buildings had two rooms, for cooking and for sleeping. The other building — two stories tall — was used mostly for storing food but also included a room where the head of the family received guests.

*A typical early Seminole village consisted of
individual houses grouped around a common area.*

Each family tended its own vegetable garden. Outside the
village, fields were planted and tended by all of the villagers
together, but shares were harvested by the families individu-
ally. These common fields stretched as far as 2 miles (3 kilome-
ters) away from the village.

Corn, beans, and squash were the most important crops planted by the Seminoles, although they also planted oranges and melons (which were first given to them by Spanish settlers), other fruits and vegetables, and tobacco. Much of what they ate was gathered from the wild rather than planted in their gardens. Their most important wild foods were potatoes and—especially—*coontie* (arrowroot), a wild plant from whose roots the Seminoles made flour. The Seminoles also gathered wild fruits and nuts.

Meat came not only from wild game, such as deer, but also from domesticated pigs, cattle, and chickens, first brought to Florida by the Spanish. Some of the early Seminoles kept very large herds of cattle.

The food most often eaten by the Seminoles was *sofki*, a very thick drink or porridge made of mashed dried corn boiled in water. At every meal sofki, either warm or cooled, was slurped up with a large spoon. Sometimes meat flavored the sofki, although more often meat was served in a separate stew. Traditionally, sofki was eaten from a common bowl, using a large, shared ladle-like sofki spoon. Sofki was usually kept simmering on the cooking fire all day for people to dip into any time they felt hungry.

William Bartram, a traveler from the north in the late 1700s, wrote this description of a meal he was given in the home of a Seminole chief:

A large bowl, with what they call "Thin drink" [sofki], is brought in and set down on a small low table; in this bowl is a great wooden ladle; each person takes up in it as much as he pleases, and after drinking until satisfied, returns it again into the bowl, pushing the handle towards the next person in the circle, and so it goes round. . . .

Bartram, a botanist, traveled all over Seminole country studying and collecting wild plants. He appreciated the generous hospitality of some of the Seminoles he met, but he didn't always find their food so agreeable. Here's his description of another Seminole banquet:

> . . . tripe soup; it is made of the belly or paunch of the beef, not overcleansed of its contents, cut and minced pretty fine, and then made into a thin soup, seasoned well with salt and aromatic herbs; but the seasoning not

A Seminole child shows off two carved sofki spoons used for eating porridge from a shared bowl.

quite strong enough to extinguish its original savour and scent. This dish is greatly esteemed by the Indians, but is, in my judgment, the least agreeable they have amongst them.

The families in each Seminole village were closely related to one another, through their mothers. A typical village might have included several sisters and their mother, the mother's husband (likely the village's leader), and the sisters' husbands, daughters, and unmarried sons. All of the women of the village and their children belonged to the same clan, a group whose mothers were related to a common ancestor; some clans included many villages.

The married men of the village, however, did not belong to the same clan as the women. It was forbidden for Seminoles of the same clan to marry each other. When a young Seminole man married, he moved from his mother's village to his wife's village, where he was expected to build her a home. All children — boys as well as girls — were counted as members of their mother's clan and grew up in their mother's village.

Some Seminole men had more than one wife, but very few had more than two. The second wife of a Seminole man was often closely related to his first wife, sometimes a younger sister.

Seminole women were responsible for planting and harvesting crops, tending animals, preparing food, and making clothes. Most child care also was done by the women (and by older brothers and sisters), although the men instructed the older boys. Men were responsible for hunting and fishing and for defending the village and waging war.

*This painting by George Catlin shows a
Seminole boy in his hunting clothes.*

Recipe for Hominy

Corn was the Seminoles' favorite food, and hominy was one of their favorite ways to eat it. Here's how hominy is prepared:

> ½ cup dried corn (popping corn)
> 1 cup water
> ¾ teaspoon baking soda (the Seminoles used ashes from firewood)

Mix the baking soda with the water. Add the corn and soak it for 12 hours, or overnight.

After the corn has soaked, bring it to a boil in the same water it soaked in. Reduce heat and simmer for about 3 hours, or until the hulls begin to separate from the corn. (The hulls are the hard skins on the outside of the kernels of corn.)

Drain the cooked corn in a sieve, then drop it into cold water. Rub the corn gently between your fingers to remove the hulls (after so many hours of soaking and cooking the hulls will be extremely soft).

Bring the corn to a boil again in fresh water. Drain, drop into cold water, and rub gently once more, to take off any remaining bits of softened hulls.

Bring the corn to a boil one last time, in lightly salted fresh water.

Drain the corn, and it's ready to eat. You may want to season your hominy with a little salt and butter, just like popcorn.

The Seminoles were fierce warriors, who often fought among themselves as well as against other Native Americans and Spanish and English settlers.

Seminole warriors would often enslave their captured ene-mies. Slaves of the Seminoles lived much as their masters did. They were permitted to marry Seminoles, and their children were generally considered free members of the village in which they were born.

TRADING WITH THE EUROPEANS ▪ Not all of the Seminoles' relations with outsiders were warlike. Trade was also a very important part of the Seminole way of life. Some Seminoles built seaworthy cypress canoes large enough to hold two dozen men, which carried them on trading expeditions as far away as Cuba. Most often, however, the Seminoles traded at towns along the Florida coast.

From their earliest days in Florida, the Seminoles relied on Spanish and English traders to supply them with such manu-factured goods as guns and ammunition, metal pots and uten-sils, and woven cloth. These goods greatly improved the Seminoles' hunting, simplified their food preparation, and even changed the way they dressed. The men were slow to abandon their traditional buckskin, which made very sturdy, long-wearing clothes, although gradually they took to wearing cloth shirts and jackets. The Seminole women more quickly adopted the softer, easier-to-sew cotton and wool cloth, which they fashioned into long, full skirts, blouses, and shawls.

In return for the Europeans' manufactured goods, the Seminoles offered their surplus garden produce and, espe-

This sketch shows some of the changes brought to the Seminoles by European traders: guns for hunting and woven cloth for making clothes.

cially, the products of their hunting. The Seminoles were formidable hunters. In the fall and winter they would leave their villages and often travel great distances on long hunting trips, usually south, farther down the Florida peninsula. Deerskins were their most important trade item, but other products of the hunt were also valuable in trade: bearskins and bear oil, panther pelts, and dried fish and meat.

Chapter Three

SEMINOLES, SETTLERS, AND ESCAPED SLAVES

When the Seminoles first settled in northern Florida, the area was governed by Spain. North of Florida were the British colonies that eventually became the original thirteen states of the United States of America.

Fighting was frequent along the border between Spanish and British territory. Colonists (white settlers) fought other colonists, colonists fought Indians, and colonists encouraged Indians to fight Indians as well as other colonists.

In 1763, Spain decided that Florida was more trouble than it was worth. Spain gave Florida to the British, and the British governed Florida from 1763 until 1783. During those years, the Seminoles had good trading relations with English traders in Florida. They found that the English traders offered better merchandise for less money than the Spanish traders had done.

After Britain lost the American Revolution, Spain once again took control of Florida, in 1783. Relations between the white governors and the Seminoles continued to be mostly good, mainly because the Spanish governors allowed English traders to continue to trade with the Seminoles in Florida.

But trouble developed between white settlers and Seminoles, especially along the border between Florida and Georgia, where Spanish territory met the United States. Seminoles resented white settlers setting up farms on the Seminoles' hunting grounds, and white settlers accused Seminoles of stealing, especially of rustling cattle.

Seminole settlements gradually spread south, deeper into Florida. During the winter hunting season, Seminole hunters would travel the length of Florida in search of game. But always they would return to the northern part of the state to plant crops and tend cattle. At the end of the 1700s, there were no permanent Seminole settlements south of Tampa Bay.

In 1812, Britain and America went to war. Some Indians of the southeastern United States—Seminoles, Creeks, and others—sided with the Americans. Some sided with the British.

Out of this war came another war: the Creek War of 1813–14. The United States fought and defeated Indians in Georgia and Alabama. At the end of this war, many Creeks fled to northern Florida, where they joined the Seminoles. Florida's population of Seminoles tripled.

By this time, many American farmers and ranchers had their eyes on the rich farmland of northern Florida—Seminole country. They pressed the U.S. government to take control of Florida from Spain and then open up Florida for white homesteaders.

The First Seminole War (1817–1818) grew out of disputes between Seminoles and white settlers near the Florida border. United States troops who fought in this war were led by Andrew Jackson, who had also fought in the Creek War and who later

*Hundreds of Creeks were killed during the War of 1812
and the Creek War that followed. Many who survived fled
to northern Florida to join the Seminoles there.*

Seminoles attack a sloop during the First Seminole War.

became president of the United States. Jackson's troops defeated the Seminoles and drove them south, deeper into Florida.

In 1821, Spain sold Florida to the United States. The Seminoles were not at all happy with this change. They had maintained fairly good relations with the Spaniards, and they thought that they would lose land to the Americans once the new owners took over Florida.

Even more unhappy with this change were the runaway slaves from the southern United States who had found a safe haven in Spanish Florida. They lived very much as the Seminoles did—tending common fields, hunting part of the year, eating the same foods, and wearing the same kinds of clothes. The escaped slaves and their families lived in villages separate from but usually near the Seminole villages. (Black slaves purchased by the Seminoles also lived in these villages.) In fact, these villages of former slaves were often counted as Seminole villages.

Sometimes a small village of escaped slaves would give a larger Seminole village livestock or food in return for protection from slave hunters by Seminole warriors. The runaway slaves feared U.S. control of Florida. They knew that if the U.S. government captured them, it would send them back to their owners.

Seminoles and fugitive slaves alike had fought the U.S. government in the First Seminole War, but the government had been too powerful for them. In 1823, after the United States took control of Florida, the Seminoles agreed to give up 24 million acres (9,712,800 hectares) of land in northern Florida, and to move onto 5 million acres (2,023,500 hectares) set aside for them in central Florida. The Seminoles also agreed to stop protecting the runaway slaves. In return, the U.S. government agreed to pay the Seminoles for their lost land and to prevent white settlers from trespassing on their new land.

Although the Seminoles did move peaceably to the reserved land in central Florida, many were unhappy about it. One chief, Neamathla, protested bitterly:

Ever since I was a small boy I have seen the white people steadily encroaching upon the Indians, and driving them from their homes and hunting grounds. When I was a boy, the Indians still roamed undisputed over the country lying between the Tennessee River and the great sea [Gulf of Mexico] of the south, and now, where there is nothing left them but the hunting grounds in Florida, the white men covet that.

NEW HARDSHIPS ▪ The land that the Seminoles left behind in northern Florida was much better for farming and hunting than the sandy and marshy land the government offered them. They found it hard to support themselves in their new homeland. Soon, there wasn't enough to eat.

In addition, by 1830 all of the Seminoles' former homelands in northern Florida had been settled by white farmers and ranchers. White settlers headed farther south, into the Seminoles' new homeland. The U.S. government didn't keep its promise to protect the Seminoles from whites killing their wild game or stealing their livestock, or even setting up farms on Seminole land.

The U.S. government had different plans for the Seminoles. It had become official policy to remove Indians living east of the Mississippi River to reservations in the West. The fast-growing population of white settlers wanted the Indians' lands. By the 1830s many tribes had already been forced to leave their homelands and travel west.

In 1832 the government decided that it was the Seminoles' turn to move to a reservation in the West. The Seminoles would

Once the white settlers had moved onto Seminole lands,
it wasn't long before their farms took over completely.
The single homestead shown here was built on the site of
one entire Indian village near the Ochlocknee River.

be expected to share land with the relocated Creeks — who had become the Seminoles' bitter enemies over the recent years of fighting.

Some Seminoles were willing to consider moving. They were worn out, tired of fighting, and didn't see much future for themselves in the poor land of central Florida.

But most Seminoles, including some of their most important chiefs, refused even to consider moving. Instead, they fought back.

Chapter Four

THE SECOND SEMINOLE WAR

One of the Seminoles who refused to move was Osceola, a young warrior. Born in Georgia about 1800, Osceola had fled as a young boy with his mother to Florida from Alabama during the Creek War. "Osceola" is an English spelling of the Seminole name he was given as a young man, *Asi-yaholo*, which means "shout given when drinking the black drink."

By the end of 1834, the U.S. government was very anxious to move the Seminoles west as soon as possible. United States officials requested a meeting with the Seminoles' most important chief, Micanopy, and other chiefs to discuss removal.

At this meeting, the U.S. officials told the chiefs that they must sign a treaty agreeing that all the Seminoles would leave Florida for the West. Osceola and others urged the chiefs not to sign. The U.S. officials warned that any chief who did not sign would be taken off the list of chiefs officially recognized by the U.S. government, and would not be allowed to represent the Seminoles in any future dealings with the government.

There is a story that may or may not be true about Osceola's behavior at this meeting. When the chiefs were asked to

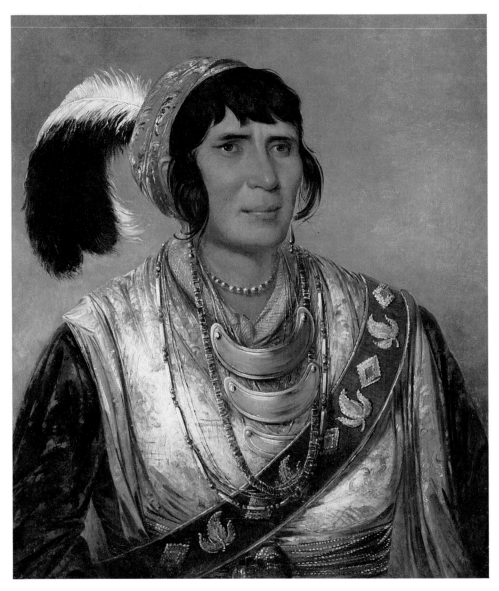

The great Seminole leader Osceola.

sign their names, Osceola took out his hunting knife and plunged it through the treaty into the table below. He declared that this was the only way he would ever sign any treaty that agreed to the Seminoles' removal from Florida.

Whether or not this actually happened, it *is* certain that Osceola strongly urged Seminole chiefs and warriors to resist the government's efforts to force them to leave Florida. In the spring of 1835, Osceola was arrested and imprisoned for speaking out against relocation. He was released after six days, when he pretended to agree to help the government convince the Seminoles to relocate.

But when he was freed, Osceola did no such thing. Instead, he continued to encourage his people's opposition to removal, and he prepared for war.

The U.S. government gave the Seminoles a deadline. All of the Seminoles remaining in Florida were to leave immediately or be prepared to leave for the West by January 1, 1836.

THE WAR BEGINS ▪ At the end of December 1835, a few days before the government's deadline, two attacks took place. Osceola and other warriors attacked a U.S. fort, killing the agent who had arrested Osceola earlier that year. And Micanopy led a larger group of warriors in a successful attack on U.S. troops. With this began the Second Seminole War, which lasted until 1842.

A few days later, Osceola led warriors in a terrible battle along the Withlacoochee River. After the battle, Osceola sent a message to the commander of the U.S. troops:

You have guns and so have we —
you have powder and lead, and so have we —
your men will fight and so will ours till the last drop
of Seminole's blood has moistened the dust of his
hunting ground.

Osceola's fierce determination, courage, and skill in leading the warriors in this battle inspired and encouraged his people. Although he was young—only in his mid-thirties—he became recognized as a leading Seminole war chief, and his opinion carried great weight at council meetings.

The Seminoles were badly outnumbered. No more than 800 Seminole warriors faced as many as 5,000 U.S. troops. They survived by hiding in the swamps and woods much of the time, trying to limit their fighting to occasions when they were most likely to be successful. During the battles, the troops took away the Seminoles' cattle and horses and destroyed any crops that were planted, but they almost never found the hidden Seminoles. The Seminoles knew the lay of the land better than anyone, so they knew the best places to hide. The only time that groups of Seminoles were likely to be caught was when captured Seminoles or their black allies led U.S. troops to their hideouts.

During the war, Osceola would not raid the homes of white settlers, and he asked his warriors not to do so, either. "It is not upon [women and children] that we make war and draw the scalping knife," he said, "it is upon men; let us act like men."

Nonetheless, during the war many homes were looted and burned, and many women and children were killed or taken hostage—by Seminoles as well as by U.S. troops and white settlers. The Seminoles—uprooted from their homes, always on the run—suffered terribly. The historian James Covington wrote:

> Some parents killed their infants when it was feared that their crying could lead the soldiers to their hiding places; some parents dug holes in the ground and placed their infants in the holes, shielded from the sun by palmetto fronds. Under cover of darkness mothers carried food and water to their babies.

THE CAPTURE OF OSCEOLA ▪ By 1837 many Seminoles—even Osceola—believed that their people could not survive another year of war. Most were still unwilling to move west, but many were ready to negotiate with the U.S. government for some sort of permanent home, perhaps in southern Florida.

Then, in September 1837, U.S. troops captured an important Seminole chief named Phillip. On October 23, 1837, under a white flag of truce, Osceola met with a U.S. general to try to negotiate Phillip's release. United States troops surrounded the place where the meeting took place, and they captured Osceola along with about eighty warriors and other Seminoles. They were put in prison at St. Augustine.

The American public was outraged at the U.S. troops' treachery. Many Americans were already angry that the government had gone to war with the Seminoles—they believed that only rich plantation owners in the South and land speculators in Florida would benefit from the war. And it was against the military code of conduct to capture or harm anyone acting

Despite the white flag that Osceola carried to the negotiations in 1837, U.S. army troops tricked him at the meeting and captured him and his followers.

honestly under an agreed-upon truce. Still, Osceola remained in prison. Some of Osceola's fellow prisoners—including Phillip's son Coacoochee ("Wildcat")—managed to escape. But Osceola was moved to Fort Moultrie, South Carolina, where he became sick. Suffering from a high fever, Osceola died—still a prisoner—on January 30, 1838.

Chapter Five

BUILDING A NEW LIFE

Osceola's death seemed to re-energize the remaining Seminole warriors. Wildcat took over Osceola's role as a war chief. But he was leading a hopeless fight. At one point Wildcat summed up his people's story:

> I was once a boy, then I saw the white man afar off. I hunted in the woods, first with a bow and arrow, then with a rifle. I saw the white man, and was told he was my enemy. I could not shoot him as I would a wolf or a bear; yet like these he came upon me; horses, cattle, and fields he took from me. He said he was my friend; he abused our women and children, and told us to go from the land. Still he gave me his hand in friendship; we took it; whilst taking it, he had a snake in the other, his tongue was forked; he lied, and stung us. I asked but for a small piece of these lands, enough to plant and to live upon far south, a spot where I could place the ashes of my kindred, a spot only sufficient upon which I could lay my wife and child. This was not

granted me. I was put in prison; I escaped. I have been again taken. . . .

It is true I have fought like a man, so have my warriors; but the whites are too strong for us. I wish now to have my band around me and go [west]. . . . I never wish to tread upon my land unless I am free.

In 1841, Wildcat surrendered. By then, most of the Seminoles had been captured or had given themselves up to be removed to the West. Seminole men, women, and children—about 4,000 altogether—were shipped from Florida to New Orleans, and from there up the Mississippi River to reserved Indian Territory in present-day Oklahoma. Captured black slaves who belonged to white U.S. citizens were returned to their owners. Other blacks who had been living among the Seminoles were sent west.

THE SEMINOLES OF OKLAHOMA ▪ The Seminoles who moved to Indian Territory in what is now Oklahoma adopted many of the white Americans' ways of living, ways that were then called "civilized." Many of the Oklahoma Seminoles became Christians. They even sent missionaries back to Florida to try to persuade the Florida Seminoles to become Christians, too.

The Seminoles of Oklahoma became one of the Five Civilized Tribes, a loosely governed organization of several of the tribes who had been forced to relocate to Oklahoma. (The other "civilized" tribes were the Cherokees, Chickasaws, Choctaws, and Creeks.) Eventually white settlers moving west demanded

This engraving, entitled "Sorrows of the Seminoles—Banished From Florida," shows the Seminoles being forced to board a ship that will take them away from their homeland.

*Putting on happy faces for the camera, Seminoles grind corn
on a reservation in Oklahoma after their removal from Florida.*

much of the tribes' land. The Seminoles and the other Native
Americans in Oklahoma were pushed onto reservations.

THE FIGHTING ENDS ▪ The fighting in Florida slowly de-
creased. On or about August 14, 1842, the U.S. government
declared that the Second Seminole War was officially over, even
though no treaty was signed to end it. The Seminoles were the
only tribe of Native Americans to come through the Indian wars
without signing a treaty making peace with the United States
government.

The Second Seminole War—the most expensive of the Indian wars—cost white settlers and the U.S. government $30 million. The Seminoles lost their homeland. About 1,600 white soldiers and civilians died during battles or from diseases and accidents connected with the fighting. At least several hundred Seminoles died, along with at least forty of their black allies.

By the time the government declared the war to be over, only about six hundred Seminoles remained in Florida, hiding in the southern Florida wetlands that no white settlers wanted. Occasional fighting continued, peaking with the Third Seminole War (1855–1858). By then, fewer than three hundred Seminoles remained in Florida.

Throughout the rest of the 1800s, after the war, the U.S. government sometimes tried to bribe the remaining Florida Seminoles to move west. The Seminoles mostly ignored these efforts. They had retreated well into the southern Florida wilderness, where they were building new lives for themselves.

NEW WAYS IN THE EVERGLADES ▪ At this time the Seminoles had no overall tribal organization. Instead, several families of the same clan would live together in a self-governing clan camp. Camps didn't come together very often. Sometimes, several camps would gather for the Green Corn Dance or for a fall hunting dance.

The Seminole's new homeland, the Everglades of southern Florida, was very different from their old lands in central and northern Florida. The Everglades is a very wide, very shallow river that flows slowly south from Lake Okeechobee in central Florida down the middle of the state to Florida Bay and the Gulf

Life in the Ever-glades was a challenge to the Seminoles, who had to find a way to build shelters and grow crops on what land they could find in the swamp.

of Mexico. This unique shallow river is covered with thick, tall, sharp-edged sawgrass. And it is dotted with hammocks — wooded islands of slightly higher, drier land sticking up out of the swampy river.

The Seminoles built their camps and planted their crops on these hammocks. They changed their way of building to make themselves more comfortable in the warmer, steamier climate of the Everglades. They lived in wooden *chickees* — huts with no

side walls, built that way to catch every cooling breeze. The chickees had palmetto-frond roofs, to keep out southern Florida's frequent thundershowers. And their floors were wooden platforms raised high—nearly 3 feet (1 meter) off the ground—to keep them dry and clear of mud. The Seminoles sometimes kept smudge fires burning (fires fueled in a way that creates a lot of thick smoke) to ward off the area's fearsome mosquitoes.

Each camp had a cookhouse that was used to cook food for everyone in the camp. The cookhouse was different from the chickees—it had a dirt floor with a raised hearth built directly on earth. The purpose of the cookhouse was to keep the cooking fire dry. Usually a pot of stew was kept simmering on the fire throughout the day.

A chickee provided little more than a roof to keep out rain and a floor to keep out mud.

A traditional Seminole cooking fire was made with four long large logs. The first log laid down pointed from the hearth to the north. The other logs pointed east, south, and west. Where all four logs met, in the hearth, the cooking fire burned. The fire was kept alive by pushing the four logs into the fire, bit by bit, as their ends burned away.

All the people living in a Seminole camp began their day with a morning meal soon after the sun came up. Most of the women spent the day at the camp, preparing food, caring for children, making clothes, and tending gardens. Some women hired themselves out as farm workers, if their camp was near a white-owned plantation. Seminole men would hunt, fish, or hire themselves out for farm work, depending on the season. In the evening, everyone would gather together at the camp for the big meal of the day. This was also the big social occasion of the day. After eating, they talked and told stories before heading off to sleep in the chickees.

There was very little land suitable for planting crops in the Everglades. The Seminoles relied more on gathering wild plants and on fishing and hunting game than they had done when they lived farther north. They raised some pigs and chickens, but found raising cattle difficult. There was too little dry land for cattle to graze, and the cattle were terribly bothered by the swarms of insects.

As they had before, the Seminoles preferred to migrate with the changing seasons. They would seek out the best land for planting crops in planting season, and the places with most plentiful game in hunting season. They traveled across the shallow water of the Everglades in canoes they carved out of solid trees.

Seminoles in the Everglades traveled by dugout canoe. Because the river is so shallow, the canoes were poled instead of paddled.

There was plenty of game for the Seminoles to hunt in the Everglades in the late 1800s: deer, bears, otters, raccoons, squirrels, rabbits, turtles, alligators, fish, birds, and even mink. Snakes were also plentiful, including deadly water moccasins and rattlesnakes, but the Seminoles avoided killing snakes and refused to eat snakemeat. They hunted for food and for furs and other goods to trade with white traders.

The Seminoles found that two products of their hunting brought especially good money from the white traders: alligator skins and feathers. Alligator skins were made into fancy leather shoes, belts, and wallets. So many alligators were killed by Seminole and white hunters that by the early 1900s very few were left alive. During this time, most of the Everglades' huge numbers of beautiful wild birds—egrets, ibis, and heron—were killed so their feathers could be used to decorate ladies' hats.

About 1900, the Seminoles' successful trading took a new turn. Many Seminole women purchased hand-cranked sewing machines from the white traders. They used these machines to create the colorful and distinctive style of dress that we now call Seminole: multicolored, carefully worked patchwork strips of cloth sewn together to make skirts for the women and long shirts for the men.

These women working at the sewing machine wear their hair in the distinctive style of the mature Seminole woman.

A young Seminole couple on their wedding day. Note the dozens of strands of pearls around the girl's neck, part of the traditional female costume.

Chapter Six

INTO THE
MODERN WORLD

The Seminoles — five hundred to six hundred of them by the early years of the twentieth century — were doing more business with white settlers than they ever had done before. But they remained very wary and suspicious of whites. Seminole children were forbidden to learn how to read and write English. And Seminoles who became friendly with whites were punished for it, often severely.

By the early 1900s, the white population of southern Florida had begun to grow. White settlers at first huddled along the coastline. But eventually they began to move inland, to land used by the Seminoles.

From the late 1920s into the Great Depression of the 1930s, more and more whites who could find no other work competed with the Seminoles for the fur trade and for game meat. But the years of good hunting were gone. The wild birds hunted for their feathers were nearly extinct. Fewer game animals were left for food and fur trading. The Seminoles and white settlers had together used up much of southern Florida's wildlife.

Wildlife—and the Seminoles' way of life—were also threatened by another development brought by white settlers: drainage. Walls were built, canals were cut, and pipes were laid to dry up wetlands and turn them into farmland, and to supply water for crops and cattle and the people of Florida's growing cities. The Everglades began to dry up and die.

When the Seminoles migrated to hunt or plant crops, they often found themselves on land now claimed by white owners. They found it harder to hunt and fish, to gather wild foods and plant gardens—to live in their traditional way.

Instead, many Seminoles found nontraditional ways to earn money while still living in traditional camps. Many worked as farm laborers. Some of the women sold handmade dolls or Seminole-style clothes. Some men hired themselves out as hunting and fishing guides. Some Seminoles even displayed their traditional-style homes to tourists, for a fee. Some built camps near tourist resorts for just this purpose.

THE MOVE TOWARD RESERVATIONS ▪ The federal government set aside reservations in southern Florida for the Seminoles and encouraged them to move there. Few were willing to move at first. The mostly Hitchiti-speaking Indians who called themselves Miccosukee had always been especially wary of the white people's government and lifestyle, and they continued to guard their independence. Gradually, "Miccosukee" became identified not only with this attitude toward the white way of living but also with a specific group of Indians. The Miccosukees lived separately from other Seminoles, mainly along the Tamiami Trail, a road built in the 1920s linking Miami and the west coast of Florida.

Seminole cowboys ride the range, herding cattle
on a reservation in southern Florida.

Then, in the 1950s, Florida's white population grew very quickly. Very little room was left for the Seminoles' traditional hunting and seasonal migration. More and more Seminoles moved to the reservations.

In 1957 the Seminole Tribe of Florida organized a tribal government. Similarly, in 1962, the group along the Tamiami Trail organized itself as the Miccosukee Tribe. Today, more than 1,500 Seminoles and Miccosukees live in Florida. (About 4,000 Seminoles live in Oklahoma, in fourteen groups, called bands, making up the Seminole Nation of Oklahoma.)

Most Seminoles today, even on the reservations, live in modern housing instead of traditional chickees. Over the past few decades it has become more common for them to live in nuclear family groups (mother, father, and their children) instead of the traditional Seminole extended family or clan camp.

Most of the Seminole reservations are located where good work is hard to find, far away from most of southern Florida's modern workplaces. Many Seminoles today are employed in seasonal farming or road construction work. Some earn a living through traditional crafts and tourist attractions. And, since the 1980s, some have found work through the bingo games now run on the reservations.

As modern as they are in many ways, the Seminoles have done less blending into mainstream American culture than many other tribes. Until recently, few Seminoles married outsiders.

Even today, some Seminoles remain proudly independent, attached to the land and to a traditional way of life. A group of perhaps two hundred of these traditional Seminoles live toward the western end of the Tamiami Trail. They refuse to move onto a government reservation, refuse to accept government aid or restrictions, and remain unattached to either "official" tribe. They hold the traditional Indian belief that no person can own

Many Seminoles today strive to maintain their traditions and to honor their heritage while living in a modern world that has not always been friendly.

the land, any more than anyone can own the sky. Guy Osceola, a traditional Seminole, explains:

> We want to be free to hunt and fish as we always did, to live here without restrictions or red tape. We want no attachment to the federal government, and no help from it. That is our right. We don't "want" [to own] land, not the way white people want it. We don't believe in ownership of a certain area.

The Miccosukee tribe has tried—not always successfully—to follow a middle path between the traditional Seminoles and the "official" Seminoles who have accepted much of the modern American way of life. Buffalo Tiger, a Miccosukee leader who adopted a modern lifestyle off the reservation, describes his people and their challenge:

> White people think that Indians are unimportant; they have never learned how to make bullets or bombs. We are "soft," according to their way. Yet we survive, because we go with nature, we can bend, we are still attached to the earth . . . .
>
> I am trying to balance between two worlds. It is very difficult; and one must be very strong.

A SEMINOLE STORY: RABBIT WHO STOLE THE FIRE

The trickster is a character found in the stories of many Native American and many African peoples. The Seminoles' trickster stories may have been influenced by African stories told to them by escaped slaves. The trickster appears in different forms in different stories. But always he fools people, and out of his mischievous troublemaking comes the lesson of the story. Here the trickster is a rabbit, much like the African-American folk character Br'er Rabbit.

■ ■ ■

The people were having a dance. Rabbit was a great singer and dancer, so they let him lead the dance. Twice Rabbit ran up to the fire and danced. The people thought he was wonderful. Then the third time Rabbit ran up to the fire he picked up a coal from the fire and ran away into the woods. He ran so fast that the people could not catch him, so they made medicine to call down rain to put out the fire Rabbit carried.

When Rabbit came back, some people said, "Don't let him lead again, because he stole the fire." But other people said,

"No, let's be generous to him. Let him lead." So they let Rabbit lead the dance, and once again he picked up a coal from the fire and ran away. Once again the people made medicine to call down rain to put out the fire.

Rabbit came back. People said, "Don't let him lead." But Rabbit's friends again got him to lead the dance. And the same thing happened all over again—only this time Rabbit found a cave in the woods where he could hide the fire so that the rain didn't put it out.

Rabbit came out of the cave a few times and set fire to grass, but the people made medicine to call down rain to put out the fire. He did this four times, and then the people saw no more fires. They thought that Rabbit was finished, that he had no more fire left.

But Rabbit still had some fire hidden in the cave. He took the fire and jumped into the ocean. He meant to swim across the ocean, carrying the fire with him.

The people saw smoke across the ocean, and they knew that Rabbit had carried the fire across the ocean and spread it around there. They were angry at Rabbit, but they couldn't reach him.

That is the way that everybody got fire.

IMPORTANT DATES

1700s   Creeks and members of other tribes settle in northern Florida, becoming the Seminoles.

1763   Spain gives Florida to Britain.

1783   Spain gets Florida back from the British, after the American Revolution.

1812   War between Britain and the United States, with Indians of the Southeast fighting on both sides.

1813–1814   Creek War in Georgia and Alabama.

1817–1818   First Seminole War, between the U.S. government and the Seminoles.

1821   Spain sells Florida to the United States.

1823   The Seminoles agree to move to central Florida.

1832   U.S. government decides to relocate all the Florida Seminoles to reserved land west of the Mississippi in Indian Territory (present-day Oklahoma).

1835	The Second Seminole War begins.
1838	Osceola dies.
1841	Wildcat surrenders.
1842	U.S. government declares the Second Seminole War to be officially ended.
1855	The Third Seminole War begins.
1858	The last of the fighting between Seminoles and the U.S. government finally ends.
1928	Tamiami Trail completed.
1950s	Many of the Seminoles remaining in the state move to reservations in southern Florida.
1957	The Seminole Tribe of Florida organizes itself as a tribal government.
1962	The Miccosukee Tribe, a group living apart from other Seminoles, organizes its tribal government.

GLOSSARY

asi. A strong herbal tea ("the black drink") drunk by Seminole men at dance ceremonies and when preparing to go to war.

chickee. An open-sided wooden hut with a raised wooden platform floor and a roof thatched with palmetto fronds.

clan. A group of families, usually living in several villages, whose women are all related to each other.

coontie. A flour made by Seminole women from the roots of a wild plant, arrowroot. Also the name for the pudding made from this flour.

hammock. A wooded island of slightly higher, drier land in the Everglades.

medicine bundle. A powerful collection of sacred tools and medicines guarded carefully by a shaman and used in ceremonies.

shaman. A leader respected for his knowledge of traditional Seminole medicine and religion.

sofki. A thick drink or porridge made of pounded dried corn cooked in water.

BIBLIOGRAPHY

*Books for children

Bartram, William. *The Travels of William Bartram: Naturalist's Edition.* Edited by Francis Harper. New Haven: Yale University Press, 1958.

Covington, James W. *The Seminoles of Florida.* Gainesville: University Press of Florida, 1993.

Derr, Mark. *Some Kind of Paradise: A Chronicle of Man and the Land in Florida.* New York: William Morrow and Co., 1989.

Douglas, Marjory Stoneman. *The Everglades: River of Grass*, revised edition. St. Simons Island, GA: Mockingbird Books, 1974.

*Garbarino, Merwyn S. *The Seminole.* New York: Chelsea House, 1989.

*Kudlinski, Kathleen V. *Night Bird: A Story of The Seminole Indians.* New York: Viking Children's Books, 1990.

*Lee, Martin. *The Seminoles.* New York: Franklin Watts, 1989.

Levitas, Gloria, Frank R. Vivelo, and Jacqueline J. Vivelo, eds. *American Indian Prose and Poetry: We Wait in the Darkness.* New York: G. P. Putnam's Sons, 1974.

*Mancini, Richard E. *Indians of the Southeast.* New York: Facts on File, 1991.

Matthiessen, Peter. *Indian Country.* Chapter 2: "The Long River." New York: Viking, 1984.

Neill, Wilfred T. *The Story of Florida's Seminole Indians.* St. Petersburg: Great Outdoors Association, 1976.

INDEX

Page numbers in *italics* refer to illustrations.

Alligators, 49
American Revolution, 25
Apalachee tribe, 12
Asi, 10

Bartram, William, 18–19

Calusa tribe, 12
Canoes, 47, *48*
Catlin, George, *13*, *21*
Cherokee Indians, 40
Chickasaw Indians, 40
Chickees, 44–46, *46*, 54
Choctaw Indians, 40
Clans, 20, 54
Clothing, 23, 49
Coontie, 18
Corn, 9, 10, 12
Covington, James, 37
Creek Indians, 15, 26, 32, 40

Creek War, 26
Crops, 18

Diseases, 12, 43

European traders, 23–25, *24*
Everglades, 43–49, *44–45*, *48*, 51–52

Families, 16–17, 20, 54
Feathers, 49, 51
First Seminole War, 26, *28*, 29
Five Civilized Tribes, 40
Food, 18–20, 22, 46

Games, 14
Green Corn Dance, 9–12, *10*

Hammocks, 44
Hitchiti language, 16, 52
Hominy, 22
Housing, 16, *17*, 44–45, 54
Hunting, 24, 48–49, 51

Jackson, Andrew, 26, 28

Language, 16

Marriage, 20, *50*
Medicine bundle, 12
Micanopy, 33, 35
Miccosukee tribe, 52, 54, 56
Muskogee language, 16

Naming ceremony, 11
Neamathla, 29–30

Oklahoma, 40, 42, *42*, 54
Osceola, 33, *34*, 35–39, *38*

Phillip, 37
Pole ball game, 14

Reservations, 52–54, 56

Second Seminole War, 35–40, 42–43
Seminole Indians
  clothing of, 23, 49
  European traders and, 23–25, *24*
  in Everglades, 43–49, *44–45*, *48*, 51–52
  families, 16–17, 20, 54
  First Seminole War, 26, *28*, 29
  food of, 18–20, 22, 46

Seminole Indians (*continued*)
  games of, 14
  Green Corn Dance, 9–12, *10*
  housing of, 16, *17*, 44–45, 54
  hunting by, 24, 48–49, 51
  language of, 16
  in Oklahoma, 40, 42, *42*, 54
  relocation of, 30, 32, 33, 35, 40, *41*
  on reservations, 52–54, 56
  Second Seminole War, 35–40, 42–43
  Third Seminole War, 43
  U.S. government and, 26, 28–30, 32, 33, 35–38, 42, 43
  women, 11, 12, 20, 47, *49*
Shamans, 11, 12
Slaves, 23, 29, 40
Sofki, 18–19, *19*

Tamiami Trail, 52, 54
Third Seminole War, 43
Timucua tribe, 12
Trickster stories, 57–58

U.S. government, 26, 28–30, 32, 33, 35–38, 42, 43

War of 1812, 26
Wildcat, 38–40
Withlacoochee River, Battle of, 35
Women, 11, 12, 20, 47, *49*